Habit Reversal

A 30-Minute Guide for Absolute Beginners to Break Bad Habits and Cultivate Positive Ones

copyright © 2023 Henry Lee

All rights reserved No part of this book may be reproduced, or stored in a retrieval system, or transmitted in any form or by any means, electronic, mechanical, photocopying, recording, or otherwise, without express written permission of the publisher.

Disclaimer

By engaging with this disclaimer, you acknowledge and accept its terms in entirety. If you do not agree with this disclaimer, please refrain from reading the guide.

The content within this guide is presented solely for informational and educational purposes and should not be construed as independent medical or professional advice. The author is not a doctor, physician, nurse, mental health provider, or registered nutritionist/dietician. Consequently, utilizing and perusing this guide does not establish any form of a physician-patient relationship.

For any concerns or inquiries regarding medical conditions, it is imperative to consult with a qualified health professional or physician. Never disregard or delay seeking professional medical advice based on the information found in this guide. The content herein is not intended to substitute any medical advice provided by a licensed and qualified medical professional.

While the information in this guide has been compiled from various sources, the author cannot guarantee the accuracy of each source and is not liable for any errors or omissions.

You acknowledge that the guide's publisher will not be held responsible for any loss or damage incurred as a result of the guide or reliance on its information. Furthermore, you agree that you assume all risk and responsibility for any actions taken in response to the guide's information.

Using this guide does not guarantee specific outcomes (e.g., weight loss or a cure). By reading this guide, you acknowledge the absence of guarantees for any particular result or expectation.

All product names, plans, or names mentioned in this guide are for identification purposes only and remain the property of their respective owners. The use of these names does not imply endorsement. Other trademarks cited herein belong to their respective owners.

In cases where cover images feature individuals, they are stock photography models, and the publisher has obtained the rights to use the images through license agreements with third-party stock image companies.

Table of Contents

Disclaimer
Table of Contents
Introduction
Chapter 1: Understanding Habits
    The Science Behind The Habit Formation
    Types of Habits
    Why are Habits Hard To Break?
    The Habit Loop
Chapter 2: The Importance of Good Habits
    Benefits of Good Habits
    Real-life Examples of Successful People with Strong Positive Habits
    How Good Habits Contribute to Mental and Physical Health
Chapter 3: The Dangers of Bad Habits
    How Bad Habits Can Negatively Impact Your Life
    Common Bad Habits and Their Consequences
    Therapies for Overcoming Bad Habits
Chapter 4: How to Identify Your Bad Habits
    Self-Reflection and Awareness
    Keeping a Habit Journal
    Identifying Triggers and Patterns
Chapter 5: Strategies to Break Bad Habits
    Replacing Bad Habits with Good Ones
    Using Tools and Apps for Habit Tracking
    Role of Support System and Professional Help
    Dealing with Setbacks and Relapses
Chapter 6: How to Cultivate Good Habits
    Setting SMART Goals
    Habit Stacking and Chaining

Maintaining Consistency and Patience
Celebrating Small Victories
Chapter 7: Overcoming Challenges in Habit Change
Common Challenges and How to Overcome Them
The Role of Mindset in Habit Change
Dealing with Lack of Motivation or Discipline
Long-term Maintenance of Good Habits
Conclusion
FAQs
Resources and Helpful Links

Introduction

Are you tired of your old habits holding you back? Are you yearning to make a positive change in your life but find yourself stuck in the same old routine day in and day out? If so, you are not alone. Millions of people around the world struggle with habits that are less than desirable, often feeling like they're running on autopilot with little control over their actions. But what if we told you there's a way to take back control and cultivate habits that align with your goals and aspirations? Welcome to our comprehensive Habit Guide!

Every day, we are driven by our habits. These repetitive actions, thoughts, or feelings shape who we are and how we experience life. They can either propel us towards our dreams or keep us shackled to our comfort zones. Our habits dictate our productivity levels, impact our physical health, and even determine our happiness quotient. It's high time we stop underestimating their power.

In this Habit Guide, we will delve into the intricate science of habit formation, breaking down complex psychological concepts into simple, understandable terms. We'll explore why we do what we do and how we can harness the power of habit to lead more fulfilling lives. You'll learn about the Habit Loop, a groundbreaking concept that reveals the secret behind every habit's existence and provides insights into how we can make or break any habit.

Imagine waking up each morning feeling invigorated and ready to conquer the day. Imagine replacing your unhealthy eating habits with nourishing ones, or swapping your chronic procrastination with consistent productivity. How would it feel to be in control of your actions, to live intentionally rather than reactively? That's the power of understanding and manipulating your habits, and that's precisely what this guide aims to help you achieve.

In this guide, we will talk about the following:

- Understanding Habits
- The Science Behind The Habit Formation
- Why are Habits Hard To Break?
- The Habit Loop
- The Importance of Good Habits
- Real-life Examples of Successful People with Strong Positive Habits
- How Good Habits Contribute to Mental and Physical Health
- The Dangers of Bad Habits
- How to Identify Your Bad Habits
- Strategies to Break Bad Habits
- How to Cultivate Good Habits
- Overcoming Challenges in Habit Change

So, are you ready to embark on this transformative journey? Are you prepared to unlock your potential by mastering your habits? If yes, then read on. This guide is designed for individuals who are ready to take charge of their lives and make meaningful changes. We promise that by the end of this guide, you'll not only understand your habits better but also possess the tools and strategies to alter them as per your desire.

Keep reading as we dive deeper into the fascinating world of habits, and together, let's pave the way for a more empowered and intentional life.

So, let's get started! Your journey towards better habits and a better life begins here.

Chapter 1: Understanding Habits

A habit is a routine of behavior that is repeated regularly and tends to occur subconsciously. In simpler terms, it's something you do so often it becomes second nature, and you don't even have to think about doing it. Habits can be anything from brushing your teeth when you wake up in the morning, to checking social media right before you go to sleep at night.

Habits are formed through a process called "habit loop," which consists of three elements: a cue, a routine, and a reward. The cue triggers the habit, the routine is the behavior you automatically engage in, and the reward is the benefit you receive from the behavior.

For instance, imagine you have a habit of drinking a cup of coffee every morning. The cue might be waking up, the routine is brewing and drinking the coffee, and the reward could be the burst of energy you get from the caffeine.

Understanding this habit loop is the key to forming new beneficial habits or changing existing ones. By manipulating the cue and the reward, you can guide your behavior in the direction you want.

Remember, not all habits are bad. Many habits, like exercising regularly or eating healthy, are incredibly beneficial. The goal isn't to eliminate all habits, but rather to ensure that your habits are working for you, not against you.

The Science Behind The Habit Formation

At its core, a habit is a series of actions that you perform regularly and automatically, often without thought. This automaticity is what distinguishes habits from other types of behaviors.

Habit formation **involves several parts of the brain, notably the prefrontal cortex and the basal ganglia.** The prefrontal cortex is involved in planning complex cognitive behavior and decision-making, while the basal ganglia play a key role in the development of emotions, habits, and pattern recognition.

When you first start doing an activity, your prefrontal cortex is heavily involved. You're making decisions, figuring out how things work, and generally paying a lot of attention to what you're doing. However, as you repeat the activity, it gradually becomes more automatic, and the basal ganglia take over. This leaves your prefrontal cortex free to do other things, which is why you can do **habitual tasks "without thinking."**

Habits are formed and strengthened through a process known as **Hebbian learning, named after Donald Hebb who proposed the theory.** It's often summarized as **"neurons that fire together wire together."** In essence, the more often you perform a behavior, the stronger the neural connections for that behavior become, making it easier and more automatic over time.

Dopamine, a neurotransmitter associated with feelings of pleasure and reward, also plays a critical role in habit formation. When you perform a behavior that leads to a rewarding outcome, your brain releases dopamine. This creates a sense of pleasure, reinforcing the behavior and making it more likely to be repeated.

Finally, **there's the concept of 'chunking'.** Your brain likes efficiency and will try to streamline frequent sequences of actions by 'chunking' them together into one single, automatic routine. This is why complex behaviors (like driving a car) can eventually become second nature, as they've been 'chunked' into a habit.

So, in essence, the science of habit formation involves repeated behaviors that strengthen neural connections, reward systems that reinforce these behaviors, and cognitive efficiency mechanisms that streamline sequences of actions. Understanding these principles can help us form good habits and break bad ones.

Types of Habits

Types of Habits: A Closer Look at Healthy vs. Unhealthy, Conscious vs. Unconscious, and Keystone Habits

Habits, the routines that govern our everyday actions, can be broadly categorized into three types: healthy vs. unhealthy habits, conscious vs. unconscious habits, and keystone habits. Each of these plays a unique role in shaping our behaviors and, ultimately, our lives.

Firstly, let's examine **healthy and unhealthy habits**. Healthy habits are those that contribute positively to our physical, emotional, and mental well-being. These may include practices like maintaining a balanced diet, regular exercise, adequate sleep, and positive thinking. For instance, someone might develop a habit of going for a morning run or eating a fruit salad for breakfast. These habits, when consistently practiced, lead to improved health, increased energy levels, and a generally better quality of life.

Conversely, unhealthy habits are those that negatively impact our health and well-being. These might include excessive consumption of junk food, lack of physical activity, smoking, or negative self-talk. Unhealthy habits often provide immediate gratification but lead to long-term detrimental effects on health and happiness. For example, regularly consuming fast food may provide instant satisfaction, but over time, it can lead to weight gain and health issues.

Next, we move on to **conscious and unconscious habits**. Conscious habits are those we deliberately decide to adopt and require effort and attention to maintain. An example could be consciously deciding to meditate for ten minutes each day. On the other hand, unconscious habits are those we perform automatically, without needing to think about them. These habits are deeply ingrained in our routines, like brushing our teeth first thing in the morning or checking our phones as soon as we wake up.

Finally, we have **keystone habits**. These are habits that, once established, can trigger a cascade of other positive behaviors. They're called 'keystones' because, much like the keystone in an arch holds all other stones in place, these habits help to hold our life in balance and encourage a series of good decisions. For example, regular exercise is often a keystone habit. It not only improves physical health but can also lead to healthier eating, better sleep, increased productivity, and improved mood. Similarly, maintaining a daily journal can be a keystone habit that encourages self-reflection, goal-setting, and mindfulness.

Understanding these different types of habits – healthy vs. unhealthy, conscious vs. unconscious, and keystone habits – is vital. This knowledge empowers us to consciously cultivate beneficial habits that enhance our well-being and happiness while working to change those habits that hold us back. Everyone has the capacity to transform their habits and, by extension, their lives. It's a journey that requires patience, effort, and consistency, but the rewards are well worth it.

Why are Habits Hard To Break?

Habits are hard to break because they are deeply wired into our brains. They form through a process called habituation, where our brains learn to perform certain actions automatically in response to specific cues. This is part of the brain's strategy to save energy and make daily tasks more efficient.

Here are a few reasons why habits can be tough to break:

- **Neurological Patterns**: When we repeat an action frequently, our brain starts to create a neurological

pattern. These patterns become more and more automatic over time, making the habit harder to break.
- **Rewards System**: Habits often have a reward associated with them, which reinforces the behavior. For example, the habit of eating junk food might be reinforced by the pleasure of taste. Overcoming this reward system can be challenging.
- **Environment and Triggers**: Our environment often triggers our habits. For instance, seeing a couch might trigger the habit of watching TV. Changing these environmental cues can be difficult, especially if they are a regular part of our day-to-day life.
- **Psychological Comfort**: Habits provide a sense of familiarity and comfort. Breaking them can cause discomfort or stress, which makes us more likely to revert back to our old behaviors.
- **Lack of Awareness**: Sometimes, we are not even aware that we are performing a habit. This lack of consciousness about our own behavior can make it very difficult to change.

Despite these challenges, it's important to remember that habits can be changed. It requires conscious effort, patience, and consistency, but with time and practice, we can replace negative habits with positive ones.

The Habit Loop

The "Habit Loop" is a concept that was popularized by Charles Duhigg in his book "The Power of Habit". It's a cycle that explains how habits work and consists of three components: Cue, Routine, and Reward.

1. **Cue**: The cue is the trigger that initiates the habit. It's a signal to your brain to go into automatic mode and choose which habit to use. Cues can be anything that triggers the habit. They can be external, such as a location, time of day, other people, or a preceding event. They can also be internal, like a particular emotion, a physical feeling, or a thought.
2. **Routine**: The routine is the behavior itself, which can be physical, mental, or emotional. This is what we usually think of when we talk about habits. For example, brushing your teeth every morning after waking up, going for a run before work, or checking your phone when you get a notification.
3. **Reward**: The reward is the positive reinforcement that strengthens the habit loop. It's the reason why your brain decides whether this particular loop is worth remembering for the future. The reward could be a physical sensation (like the taste of a cookie or the endorphin rush after a workout), emotional pay-off (feeling of accomplishment), or even just the reduction of a craving. Over time, this process becomes automatic and the cue and reward become intertwined until a powerful sense of anticipation and craving emerges.

Understanding the habit loop is crucial because it provides a framework for understanding how habits work, which is the first step towards changing them. By identifying the cues and rewards that drive your habits, you can start to change the routine or respond to the same cue with a different routine. This is the essence of habit change according to the Habit Loop concept.

Chapter 2: The Importance of Good Habits

Good habits are the foundation of a successful and fulfilling life. They influence our physical health, mental well-being, productivity, relationships, and personal growth. Understanding their importance is key to achieving our goals, maintaining balance, and ultimately, shaping our destiny. Let's delve into why good habits matter so much.

Benefits of Good Habits

Good habits have the power to significantly improve our lives, contributing to our physical, mental, and emotional well-being. Here are some of the key benefits of cultivating good habits:

Improved Physical Health

Regular exercise, a balanced diet, and adequate sleep are all important habits to maintain good physical health. By engaging in regular exercise, one can maintain a healthy weight, improve cardiovascular health, and reduce the risk of developing chronic diseases such as diabetes, cancer, and heart disease.

A balanced diet is essential for providing our bodies with the necessary nutrients and energy to function optimally. Adequate sleep helps to restore and rejuvenate our bodies, aid in memory consolidation, improve mood, and reduce the risk of obesity, diabetes and cardiovascular disease. Good habits are essential for promoting longevity and overall physical health.

Mental Health Enhancement

Engaging in good habits such as mindfulness, meditation, or daily relaxation can provide numerous mental health benefits. By regularly practicing these habits, individuals can experience reduced symptoms of anxiety and depression, increased mood, heightened focus, concentration, and better cognitive function.

Studies have also found that regular mindfulness and relaxation practices can enhance brain function and physical health, leading to a more satisfied and healthier life overall. Incorporating these habits into a daily routine can lead to positive improvements in mental and physical health, ultimately providing a more fulfilling and happier life.

Better Productivity

Good habits related to time management, organization, and task prioritization provide a significant boost to productivity. One of the key benefits of these habits is that they free up valuable mental resources that can be used for more complex tasks. This is because automating certain decisions, such as how and when to start your workday, reduces decision fatigue and allows you to focus on tasks that require higher levels of cognitive functioning.

By setting clear goals and priorities, you can also reduce the amount of time spent on low-priority tasks, enabling you to allocate resources more effectively. Additionally, prioritizing tasks helps in better time management, which then further enhances productivity. Therefore, developing good habits in these areas can lead to increased productivity and overall success in whatever task or job you undertake.

Stronger Relationships

Active listening, expressing gratitude, and regular communication are not only healthy habits but also key to stronger relationships. Active listening helps individuals fully understand the other person, their thoughts, feelings, and perspectives, leading to empathy and mutual respect. Expressing gratitude can improve the overall mood of the loved one.

Consistent communication can help prevent misunderstandings, conflicts, and strengthen bonds. Good habits promote trust, honesty, and positivity, ultimately leading to a happier and more fulfilling relationship.

Personal Growth

Good habits, such as reading, lifelong learning, or pursuing a hobby, bring about various benefits, including personal growth. One of the benefits is knowledge expansion, which allows individuals to remain informed and up-to-date with current trends, events, and discoveries. These habits also stimulate creativity, encouraging individuals to think outside the box and generate innovative ideas.

Additionally, they contribute to increased self-confidence as individuals learn new skills and discover hidden talents, boosting their sense of achievement and self-worth. Therefore, cultivating good habits is essential for personal growth and overall well-being.

Financial Stability

Developing good financial habits, such as regular saving, sensible spending and thoughtful investing, can lead to a multitude of benefits for an individual. One of the most crucial benefits is financial stability and independence. By practicing these habits, an individual can build wealth over time, making them less reliant on external factors like loans.

It also prepares them for emergencies by having a cushion of savings to fall back on. Additionally, this helps an individual secure their financial future by ensuring that they have adequate savings for retirement and other future goals. By making informed and sustainable financial choices, an individual can not only maintain but also amplify their financial well-being.

Improved Self-Discipline

Developing good habits not only leads to a healthier and happier lifestyle, but it also improves self-discipline. Self-discipline is the ability to control one's behavior and impulses to achieve goals. With better self-discipline, individuals can more easily resist temptations that may hinder progress toward their goals. This skill also allows individuals to consistently work towards their objectives, leading to greater achievement and success in various aspects of life. By forming good habits, individuals can enhance their self-discipline, leading to long-term benefits.

Happiness

Good habits bring a multitude of benefits to one's life, and one of the most significant ones is increased happiness. By cultivating good habits that align with personal goals and values, individuals can experience a sense of fulfillment and satisfaction. For instance, the habit of regular exercise leads to the release of endorphins, promoting a positive mood and reducing stress levels.

Additionally, adherence to good financial habits, such as budgeting and saving, can provide a sense of security and peace of mind. Highlighting the importance of good relationships, being in tune with family and friends brings a sense of belonging and support, contributing to long-term happiness. Overall, good habits can transform one's well-being and foster a happier, healthier life.

Remember, the power of a good habit lies in its consistency. It's not what we do occasionally that shapes our lives, but what we do consistently.

Real-life Examples of Successful People with Strong Positive Habits

Success is often a result of consistent positive habits, and this becomes clear when we take a look at the daily routines of some of the world's most successful individuals.

1. **Bill Gates**: The co-founder of Microsoft is an avid reader, often consuming a book a week. This habit has helped him gain a broad range of knowledge and insights, contributing to his innovative thinking.
2. **Elon Musk**: Known for his extraordinary work ethic, the CEO of Tesla and SpaceX often works up to 100 hours a week. This dedication showcases his habit of perseverance and hard work.
3. **Warren Buffett**: As one of the most successful investors globally, Buffett spends a significant portion of his day reading. This continuous learning habit has been a major factor in his financial acumen and success.
4. **Oprah Winfrey**: The media mogul begins each day with meditation. This habit of mindfulness helps her maintain a sense of peace and focus, contributing to her emotional well-being and success.
5. **Mark Zuckerberg**: The Facebook founder sets personal challenges for himself every year, pushing him to learn new things and grow beyond his work. This goal-setting habit encourages constant improvement and innovation.
6. **Richard Branson**: The founder of the Virgin Group prioritizes his health, waking up early to exercise before starting his workday. This habit boosts his energy levels and productivity, contributing to his entrepreneurial success.

These examples demonstrate how good habits can significantly influence one's success, from enhancing knowledge and work ethic to promoting mindfulness and health.

How Good Habits Contribute to Mental and Physical Health

The journey towards achieving optimal health is often paved with the bricks of good habits. These habits, which serve as the foundation of our lifestyle, significantly impact both our physical and mental well-being. Here are some key habits that contribute to a healthy life:

- **Regular Exercise:** Regular physical activity is a cornerstone of good health. It strengthens our muscles, improves cardiovascular health, and enhances our energy levels. Beyond its physical benefits, exercise also contributes to our mental well-being, serving as a natural stress reliever, mood enhancer, and confidence booster.
- **Adequate Sleep:** Sleep is integral to our body's healing and rejuvenation process. It provides the necessary downtime for our bodies to repair cellular damage and for our minds to process the day's experiences. Good sleep habits can lead to improved focus, better emotional regulation, and reduced risk of various health issues.
- **Balanced Nutrition:** Consuming a balanced diet rich in essential nutrients is critical for our physical health, contributing to energy production, weight management, and disease prevention. Moreover,

certain foods can also influence our mental health by impacting our mood and cognitive function.
- **Social Interaction:** Fostering strong social connections provides us with a sense of belonging and emotional support. This habit not only enriches our lives but also bolsters our mental resilience, helping us navigate life's ups and downs more effectively.
- **Mindfulness and Meditation:** Practicing relaxation techniques such as mindfulness and meditation can help manage stress, reduce anxiety, and enhance mental clarity. These practices promote a sense of peace and well-being, contributing significantly to our mental health.
- **Positive Outlook:** Maintaining a positive outlook can significantly influence our perception of ourselves and the world around us. This habit can help us overcome challenges, improve our resilience, and lead to better mental health.

Good habits are much more than simple routines; they are powerful tools that, when consistently applied, can significantly improve our physical and mental health.

Chapter 3: The Dangers of Bad Habits

Bad habits, often dismissed as minor nuisances, can have profound implications on our overall health and well-being. From affecting our physical health to impairing our mental state, these harmful patterns of behavior can gradually erode the quality of our lives.

How Bad Habits Can Negatively Impact Your Life

Understanding the detrimental effects of bad habits is crucial as they can silently infiltrate various aspects of our lives, causing significant harm to the following;

- **Physical Health:** Habits like smoking, excessive alcohol consumption, and unhealthy eating can lead to several health issues, including heart disease, liver damage, obesity, and diabetes. Lack of physical activity can also lead to weight gain and reduced stamina.
- **Mental Health:** Habits such as excessive screen time or substance abuse can contribute to mental health conditions like depression, anxiety, and stress. Even seemingly harmless habits like procrastination can lead to increased stress and reduced self-esteem.
- **Relationships:** Bad habits can strain relationships. For example, constantly being late can cause others to view you as unreliable, while habits like constant criticism can push people away.
- **Productivity and Success:** Habits like procrastination, disorganization, and constantly checking social media

can reduce productivity, hamper your performance at work or school, and limit your potential for success.
- **Financial Health:** Some bad habits can be financially draining. Impulsive shopping, gambling, or frequently eating out can lead to financial instability.

In essence, while we may overlook or downplay our bad habits, they can have significant negative impacts on multiple aspects of our lives. It's crucial to identify and work on eliminating these harmful patterns to improve our quality of life.

Common Bad Habits and Their Consequences

Bad habits, while often overlooked, can significantly impact various aspects of our lives. Some of the most common ones include:

- **Unhealthy Eating:** Consuming junk food or overeating can lead to obesity and other health issues like diabetes and heart disease.
- **Smoking and Excessive Alcohol Consumption:** These habits can cause a plethora of health problems, from lung cancer and heart disease to liver damage and mental health disorders.
- **Lack of Physical Activity:** A sedentary lifestyle can lead to weight gain, decreased stamina, and increased risk of several diseases.
- **Procrastination:** This habit can lead to increased stress, reduced self-esteem, and lower productivity. It can also negatively affect your professional growth and success.

- **Poor Sleep Habits:** Not getting enough sleep or having irregular sleep patterns can lead to physical fatigue, impaired cognitive function, and mental health issues like depression and anxiety.
- **Excessive Screen Time:** Spending too much time on electronic devices can lead to eye strain, sleep disturbances, and mental health problems. It can also reduce productivity and physical activity.
- **Impulsive Shopping or Gambling:** These habits can lead to financial instability and stress.

It's important to recognize these habits and their potential consequences. By taking steps to break them, you can improve your health, relationships, productivity, and overall quality of life.

Therapies for Overcoming Bad Habits

Overcoming damaging habits is not an easy feat. It requires determination, resilience, and a strong will. Here are some examples of individuals who have successfully overcome their bad habits:

1. Cognitive Behavioral Therapy (CBT): Cognitive Behavioral Therapy (CBT) is a highly effective method for overcoming bad habits. It works by identifying and restructuring harmful thoughts that influence behavior. For example, a CBT therapist can help someone who overeats when stressed to find alternative coping mechanisms, such as walking or meditation.

2. Hypnotherapy: Hypnotherapy is a therapy technique that uses guided relaxation to create a trance-like state of heightened focus. This allows individuals to concentrate on specific tasks or thoughts, aiding in breaking bad habits like smoking or nail-biting.

3. Mindfulness-Based Cognitive Therapy (MBCT): Mindfulness-Based Cognitive Therapy (MBCT) merges mindfulness techniques with cognitive therapy. By non-judgmentally observing thoughts and feelings, individuals can alter their reactions to urges related to bad habits, helping them choose not to act on these impulses.

4. Dialectical Behavior Therapy (DBT): Dialectical Behavior Therapy (DBT) is a type of cognitive-behavioral therapy that teaches behavioral skills to help people handle stress better, manage their emotions, and improve their relationships. It can be particularly effective for individuals whose bad habits are linked to emotional instability or interpersonal difficulties.

5. Motivational Interviewing: This is a therapeutic technique that aids individuals in dealing with mixed emotions and doubts to discover the inner drive required to modify their actions. This method is frequently employed in addiction treatment and can be highly beneficial in assisting people to break free from detrimental habits.

6. Exposure Therapy: Exposure Therapy is a psychological treatment designed to help individuals confront their fears. Over time, avoidance of fear can intensify it. 'Habit reversal training,' a form of exposure therapy, helps people become aware of their habits and understand their behavior triggers and effects.

7. Acceptance and Commitment Therapy (ACT): Acceptance and Commitment Therapy (ACT) combines mindfulness with behavior-change strategies. It aids in overcoming bad habits by promoting acceptance of thoughts and feelings, instead of battling or feeling guilt over them.

Overcoming bad habits often requires professional help. Therapies like Exposure Therapy, MBCT, and ACT can aid in breaking harmful behaviors. Persistence and tailored approaches are key to improving one's quality of life.

Chapter 4: How to Identify Your Bad Habits

Identifying bad habits is the first step towards self-improvement. These deeply ingrained patterns, often overlooked, can hinder our growth. Whether it's procrastination, unhealthy eating, or excessive screen time, recognizing these habits is crucial. This guide will help spotlight your damaging habits and kickstart your journey towards change.

Self-Reflection and Awareness

Self-reflection and awareness are indeed pivotal in the journey of personal growth. These twin pillars involve stepping back from the whirlwind of daily life, taking a good, hard look at your actions, thoughts, and emotions, and deriving valuable insights into your habits. By cultivating self-awareness, you unlock the ability to understand the 'why' behind your actions, which is the first step towards meaningful change.

It's all too easy to cruise through life on autopilot, never questioning why you stick to specific routines or fall into certain patterns. But if you want to grow, to improve, to break free from the shackles of unhelpful habits, awareness is crucial. It calls for honest introspection and the courage to face parts of yourself that may not be particularly flattering.

Imagine being in a car. As the driver, you have control, but only if you're aware of your surroundings, your vehicle's condition, and your destination. Similarly, self-awareness puts you in the driver's seat of your life.

So, how do you cultivate this awareness? Start with self-questioning. Ask yourself: What are the things I repeatedly do, even when I'm fully aware they aren't beneficial for me? Why do I persist in these actions? How do I feel before, during, and after these actions? What consequences do they have on my life, my well-being, my relationships, and my goals?

The answers to these questions might surprise you. They will shed light on the habits you need to change, and the patterns you need to break. They will show you where you're stuck and where you need to go.

Remember, self-awareness isn't just about identifying what you're doing wrong. It's also about recognizing what you're doing right. It's about understanding your strengths, your values, and your passions, and leveraging them to build healthier habits and a happier life.

Self-reflection and awareness are not one-time actions; they're ongoing processes. They require patience, persistence, and kindness towards yourself. But rest assured, the rewards are well worth the effort. By harnessing the power of self-reflection and awareness, you'll be better equipped to ditch those pesky bad habits and replace them with ones that propel you toward your true potential.

Keeping a Habit Journal

A habit journal is a powerful tool in identifying bad habits. It involves keeping a record of your daily activities and reflecting on them. This process can help uncover patterns and habits that might otherwise go unnoticed.

Start by recording everything you do throughout the day, including the time spent on each activity. Don't judge or try to change anything at this point - just observe. Do this for a week or two, and patterns will start to emerge. You may find that you're spending more time on social media than you thought, or that you tend to snack when you're bored.

The act of writing down your activities can also increase your awareness. It forces you to pay attention to what you're doing, which can help you identify habits that don't serve you well.

Identifying Triggers and Patterns

Once you've developed self-awareness and kept a habit journal, the next step is to identify triggers and patterns. Triggers are events, feelings, or situations that prompt you to engage in a particular habit. Patterns, on the other hand, are recurring sequences of behavior that often follow triggers.

For instance, if you notice that you tend to eat junk food when you're stressed, then stress is a trigger, and eating junk food is a pattern. Identifying these can help you understand the root cause of your bad habits.

To identify triggers, review your habit journal and look for commonalities before engaging in a bad habit. Do you always have a cigarette after a meal? Do you binge-watch TV when you're feeling lonely? These triggers can be external (like certain people or places) or internal (like emotions or thoughts).

Once you've identified your triggers, look for patterns. Are there specific times of day when you engage in the habit? Do you tend to do it more when you're with certain people or in certain situations?

Identifying bad habits involves self-reflection and awareness, keeping a habit journal, and identifying triggers and patterns. This process may be challenging, but it's crucial for personal growth and change. Remember, the goal isn't to judge yourself or feel guilty, but to understand your habits so you can take steps towards changing them.

Chapter 5: Strategies to Break Bad Habits

Breaking bad habits is a challenging but rewarding journey. It involves replacing bad habits with good ones, utilizing tools and apps for habit tracking, seeking the help of a supportive community, and handling setbacks and relapses. Each step requires determination, patience, and self-compassion. In this guide, we'll explore these strategies in detail to help you successfully break your bad habits.

Replacing Bad Habits with Good Ones

A powerful strategy to break free from bad habits isn't merely about stopping them, it's about replacing them with good ones. It's crucial to understand that if you simply try to stop a habit without substituting it with a healthier alternative, you'll leave a gap. This void can often lead you back to the old behavior, causing a relapse into the bad habit you're trying to kick.

Let's take an example. Imagine your bad habit is reaching for junk food when stress levels rise. Instead of just trying to resist the urge, replace it with a healthier habit. You could go for a brisk walk or practice deep breathing exercises. Both activities not only distract you from stress eating but also help to alleviate the stress itself.

Now, think about the positive habits you'd like to incorporate into your life. Start small, making sure the new habit is manageable and fits seamlessly into your routine. If you're aiming to start exercising, for instance, don't jump straight into an hour-long high-intensity workout. Begin with a short, enjoyable routine. It could be as simple as a ten-minute walk around the block or a brief yoga session.

As your body adapts and becomes more comfortable with this new routine, incrementally increase the intensity and duration. But remember, it's vital that you keep it enjoyable. If the workout becomes a chore, you're less likely to stick with it. The ultimate goal here is sustainability.

In essence, breaking bad habits is a two-step process: stop the undesirable behavior and replace it with a beneficial one. While it may seem challenging initially, with consistent effort and a positive mindset, you can successfully transform your habits and, ultimately, your life.

Using Tools and Apps for Habit Tracking

In the technologically advanced world we live in today, there's no shortage of tools and apps designed to help you track your habits. These digital aids can serve as a constant, visual reminder of your progress, providing the motivation you need to keep going strong. They can also help you identify patterns in your behavior and triggers that might lead you back into old habits, offering invaluable insights that can aid in your journey toward habit change.

Consider some of the features these apps offer. Many provide reminders, nudging you to stick to your new routines. These reminders can be particularly helpful when you're just starting out with a new habit and haven't yet formed a solid routine.

Additionally, some apps utilize the concept of "streaks," which track how many days in a row you've successfully followed your new habit. Seeing a growing streak can be incredibly motivating, creating a sense of achievement and encouraging you to maintain your progress.

Rewards are another feature often found in habit-tracking apps. By setting and reaching specific goals, you can earn rewards, making the process of forming new habits feel more like a game than a chore. This gamification can make habit formation more fun and engaging, increasing your likelihood of sticking with it.

When choosing a habit-tracking tool or app, it's important to find one that aligns with your needs and preferences. There's a plethora of options available, so take your time to find one that you find user-friendly and enjoyable to use.

Remember, though, while these tools can offer assistance, they're not magic. The real work comes from your commitment to change. The app can remind you to drink more water or take a daily walk, but it's up to you to actually do it. The tool is there to support you, but the determination, consistency, and effort must come from within. With the right mindset and a helpful tracking tool, you'll be well on your way to replacing old habits with new, healthier ones.

Role of Support System and Professional Help

Embarking on the journey to break bad habits can often feel like you're climbing a steep hill. It's a challenging process that requires commitment and willpower. However, having a robust support system at your side can significantly lighten the load and make the journey smoother and more manageable.

Your support system could encompass a variety of individuals in your life. Friends who understand your struggles, family members who care about your well-being, or peers who are also striving to break their own habits can all form part of this critical network. They can offer you encouragement when your spirits are low, share their experiences to provide you with new insights and perspectives, and importantly, hold you accountable for your actions. Knowing that others are invested in your success can give you an extra push to keep going when things get tough.

However, there may be instances where the habits you're trying to break are deeply ingrained or have addictive elements. In such cases, relying solely on your personal support system might not be enough. That's where professional help comes in. Therapists and counselors, who are specifically trained in understanding the complexities of human behavior, can provide you with the tools and strategies to tackle these stubborn habits effectively.

These professionals can help you delve deeper into your habits, understand the root causes, and identify potential triggers. With their guidance, you can develop effective strategies for change that are tailored to your specific needs and circumstances.

If you find yourself wrestling with a habit that feels beyond your control, don't hesitate to seek professional help. There's no shame in reaching out to experts. In fact, taking that step is a clear sign of strength and a testament to your determination to change. Remember, the goal is to improve your life, and sometimes, the best way to do that is by seeking assistance from those trained to help.

Dealing with Setbacks and Relapses

When you're trying to break a bad habit, encountering setbacks and relapses is a common occurrence. It's crucial to recognize that these aren't indications of failure or defeat; rather, they're integral parts of the overall process of change.

Experiencing a setback can be disheartening, but it doesn't mean that you should start berating yourself. Instead, view it as an opportunity for learning and growth. Ask yourself - what triggered the relapse? Was it a specific event, situation, or emotion? Reflecting on this can help you identify potential pitfalls and devise strategies to avoid them in the future.

Next time you're faced with a similar trigger, you'll be better equipped to handle it differently, perhaps by employing coping mechanisms or engaging in an alternative, healthier behavior.

Breaking a habit isn't something that happens overnight. It's a journey that takes time, requires patience, and demands consistent effort. It's important to keep reminding yourself of this, particularly during tough times when progress seems slow or non-existent.

Along your journey, make sure to celebrate small victories. Did you manage to resist the urge to fall back into your old habit today? That's a win. Did you reach a mini-goal you set for yourself? That's another win. These small victories are stepping stones towards your ultimate goal, and acknowledging them can boost your morale and keep you motivated.

Remember, setbacks are merely temporary obstacles, not impassable roadblocks. Keep your end goal firmly in mind, constantly remind yourself of why you want to break this habit and use any setbacks as stepping stones towards becoming a stronger, more resilient version of yourself.

Chapter 6: How to Cultivate Good Habits

Cultivating good habits is the key to personal growth and success. It's about creating routines that help you reach your goals and live a healthier, happier life. The process involves setting SMART goals, using techniques like habit stacking and chaining, maintaining consistency and patience, and celebrating small victories. This guide will walk you through these steps to help you successfully cultivate good habits.

Setting SMART Goals

Embarking on the journey of cultivating good habits starts with setting SMART goals. This acronym stands for Specific, Measurable, Achievable, Relevant, and Time-bound. Each component of this framework serves a unique purpose in guiding you toward effective habit formation.

Specificity is the first step in this process. Being specific about your goal strips away the ambiguity and provides a clear direction. Instead of stating a vague intention like "I want to exercise more", drill down to the specifics - "I will walk for 30 minutes every day". This specificity not only outlines what action you'll take, but it also sets a clear expectation that's easy to follow through on.

Measurability is the next crucial element. By making your goal measurable, you create a tangible way to track your progress. For instance, if your objective is to read more books, decide on a precise number of books you aim to read each month. This gives you a concrete target to hit and allows you to visibly see your progress, which can be incredibly motivating.

The third component is **Achievability**. While it's great to aim high, your goal should still be within your reach. Setting unrealistic goals can lead to frustration and demotivation. If you're new to running, setting a goal to run a marathon in a month might be setting yourself up for failure. Instead, start with smaller, achievable goals, like running for fifteen minutes a day. As you build stamina and confidence, you can gradually increase your goal.

Relevance is another essential factor. Your habit change should align with your broader life goals and values. If you're aiming to lead a healthier lifestyle, your habit of daily exercise or reading health-related literature becomes relevant. This alignment ensures that every small habit you're working on contributes to your larger life vision, making the process more meaningful and motivating.

Finally, your goals should be **Time-bound**. Deadlines create a sense of urgency and can spur you into action. If you want to learn a new language, set a deadline for when you want to be able to hold a basic conversation. This encourages consistent effort and keeps procrastination at bay.

In essence, setting SMART goals provides you with a clear, well-defined roadmap for your habit formation journey. It breaks down your aspirations into actionable steps and sets up a framework that enables progress, fosters motivation, and brings you closer to your ultimate objectives. With SMART goals, you're not just dreaming about the change - you're planning for it and making it happen.

Habit Stacking and Chaining

Habit stacking and chaining are effective techniques that can significantly aid you in cultivating and maintaining good habits. They work by leveraging the power of existing habits and routines, making the process of habit formation more seamless and less daunting.

Habit stacking is a technique that involves adding a new habit onto an already established one. This strategy takes advantage of the brain's tendency to create and follow patterns. By attaching a new habit to an existing one, you're essentially creating a mental link between the two actions, making it easier for your brain to adopt the new habit.

For example, if you already have an ingrained habit of enjoying a cup of coffee each morning, you could stack a new habit onto it, like meditating for 10 minutes after finishing your coffee. The existing habit (drinking coffee) acts as a trigger for the new habit (meditation). Over time, the sequence of 'drinking coffee then meditating' can become an automatic routine.

Habit chaining, also known as habit sequencing, takes this concept a step further by linking several habits together to form a routine. This chain of actions can create a powerful routine that, once established, can run on autopilot.

Consider your morning routine as an example. It could be a sequence of habits like waking up, drinking a glass of water, meditating for 10 minutes, going for a walk, and then having breakfast. Each action triggers the next, creating a habitual flow. With consistency, this chain of habits can become an automatic part of your morning.

The beauty of these techniques lies in their simplicity and effectiveness. They work because they tap into the patterns our brains naturally follow. When one action becomes automatic, it serves as a trigger for the next action in the chain or stack, making it easier to stick to your new habits.

So, as you embark on your journey of habit formation, consider integrating habit stacking and chaining into your strategy. By linking your new habits to existing ones and creating chains of habits, you can make the process more manageable and more successful. Remember, the goal is to make the new habits fit seamlessly into your lifestyle, and these techniques are powerful tools to help you do just that.

Maintaining Consistency and Patience

When it comes to habit formation, consistency and patience are your most powerful allies. They're the driving force behind every successful habit change and are fundamental to achieving your long-term goals.

Consistency, in essence, is all about regularity. It's not about executing your new habit perfectly every time, but rather about adhering to your plan as consistently as possible. The power of consistency lies in its ability to make your new habits a normal part of your routine, eventually leading to them becoming second nature.

Imagine you're aiming to cultivate a daily reading habit. Some days, you might find it easy to sit down with a book, while on others, it may feel like a struggle. The key is to stick to your plan regardless of how you feel. Even if you only manage to read a few pages, you're still maintaining the consistency of your reading habits.

If you miss a day, don't fall into the trap of self-criticism. Life happens, and there will be days when your routines get disrupted. Instead of beating yourself up, focus on getting back on track the next day. Remember, it's not the occasional missed day that hampers habit formation, but consistent neglect.

Alongside consistency, patience is equally crucial. Real, lasting change takes time. It's important to remember that habit formation isn't an overnight process. You won't suddenly become a voracious reader or a marathon runner in a week. These things take time, and expecting immediate results can lead to unnecessary frustration and disappointment.

Instead, remind yourself that progress may be slow, but each small step moves you closer to your goal. Celebrate your little victories along the way - every page you read, every mile you run. These small wins accumulate over time and contribute to substantial change.

In the journey of habit formation, be patient with yourself. Understand that you're undertaking a process of change, which takes time. As long as you're moving forward, no matter how slow or small the steps may seem, you're on the right path.

Maintaining consistency and patience in your habit formation journey helps you build resilience and perseverance. It allows you to approach your goals with a balanced perspective, understanding that the path to success is paved with regular effort and compassionate patience.

Celebrating Small Victories

Recognizing and celebrating your progress, no matter how small, plays a crucial role in the habit formation process. Each step you take towards your goal represents a triumph, a testament to your efforts and dedication, and it deserves to be celebrated.

Celebration acts as a powerful reinforcement, encouraging you to keep pushing forward. It's a way of acknowledging your hard work and rewarding yourself for it. This positive reinforcement not only boosts your motivation but also helps solidify the new habit in your routine.

Imagine you're working on developing a daily writing habit. After consistently writing for a week, take a moment to acknowledge this achievement. Celebrate your consistency, your commitment, and your progress. This celebration could be as simple as taking a few minutes at the end of the week to reflect on your accomplishments and the progress you've made.

The rewards or celebrations don't have to be grand or expensive. They should, however, be meaningful to you and bring you joy. It could be as simple as allowing yourself a few extra minutes of relaxation, treating yourself to your favorite snack, or dedicating some time to a hobby you love.

Perhaps you could create a rewards system where you treat yourself to something special after reaching certain milestones. For example, after maintaining your writing habit for a month, you could reward yourself with a new notebook or a book by your favorite author.

The key is to choose rewards that resonate with you and align with your goals. If you're working towards a fitness goal, your reward could be a new workout outfit or a healthy treat. If your goal is related to personal development, perhaps your reward could be a new book or an online course.

Remember, the aim of celebrating small victories is to reinforce your new habits and motivate you to continue on your journey. It's about acknowledging your efforts, savoring your progress, and motivating yourself to keep going. By celebrating your small victories, you're not just rewarding yourself - you're reinforcing your commitment to your goals and paving the way for continued success.

Building beneficial habits entails establishing SMART objectives, employing habit stacking and chaining techniques, upholding regularity and patience, and acknowledging minor triumphs. Keep in mind, the path to forming habits is more of a long-distance run than a quick dash. It demands commitment, endurance, and self-kindness. However, by utilizing these methods, you can effectively develop positive habits that contribute to a more wholesome and joyful existence.

Chapter 7: Overcoming Challenges in Habit Change

Change is inevitable, and so are the challenges that come along with it. The journey towards habit change, in particular, can often feel like an uphill battle, filled with numerous obstacles. However, overcoming these challenges is not impossible. It requires understanding common challenges, fostering the right mindset, and dealing with a lack of motivation or discipline.

Common Challenges and How to Overcome Them

One of the most common challenges in habit change is resistance to change. People often resist change because it's uncomfortable and requires stepping out of their comfort zones. To overcome this challenge, individuals need to understand the benefits of the change and how it aligns with their long-term goals. Visualizing the positive outcomes can inspire action and make the discomfort of change more bearable.

Another common challenge is the feeling of being overwhelmed. Changing a habit isn't easy, and trying to change several habits at once can be daunting. The key to overcoming this challenge is to start small. Focus on one habit at a time and break it down into manageable steps.

The Role of Mindset in Habit Change

Mindset plays a crucial role in habit change. A fixed mindset can hinder progress, while a growth mindset can fuel it. Those with a fixed mindset believe their abilities and habits are set in stone, which can lead to a sense of helplessness when facing challenges. On the other hand, those with a growth mindset believe they can improve and change through effort and persistence.

Cultivating a growth mindset involves changing how one thinks about failure and challenges. Instead of viewing them as insurmountable obstacles, they should be seen as opportunities for learning and growth. This shift in perspective can make the process of habit change less intimidating and more empowering.

Dealing with Lack of Motivation or Discipline

A lack of motivation or discipline can be a significant obstacle to habit change. It's easy to feel motivated and disciplined in the beginning, but these feelings can wane over time. To maintain motivation, individuals need to connect their habits to their core values and goals. This connection can provide a powerful source of motivation that can sustain them through the ups and downs of habit change.

Discipline, on the other hand, can be cultivated through practice and consistency. It's about making a commitment to change and sticking to it, even when it's difficult. Setting clear and realistic goals, developing a plan, and tracking progress can also boost discipline.

Overcoming challenges in habit change involves understanding common challenges, adopting the right mindset, and dealing with a lack of motivation or discipline. While the journey may be filled with obstacles, remember that each challenge is an opportunity for growth. With persistence, patience, and a positive mindset, anyone can successfully navigate the path of habit change.

Long-term Maintenance of Good Habits

Maintaining good habits over the long term is just as important as establishing them. This process requires regular review and adjustment, sustained motivation, and learning from those who've successfully maintained their habits.

Importance of Regular Review and Adjustment

Habits aren't set in stone; they're dynamic and require regular review and adjustment. As individuals change and grow, their habits may need to adapt to match their evolving goals and lifestyles. Regularly reviewing habits provides an opportunity to reflect on what's working, what's not, and what adjustments need to be made.

Adjusting habits doesn't mean failure; it means being responsive to change. For instance, if someone has established a habit of running every morning but finds it increasingly difficult due to changing weather conditions, they might adjust the habit to indoor exercises. This flexibility allows for the maintenance of the foundational habit – regular exercise while adapting to external factors.

Staying Motivated for Long-term Habit Maintenance

Maintaining motivation over the long term can be challenging but it's crucial for habit maintenance. One effective way to stay motivated is by setting and celebrating small, incremental goals. Each small victory can boost motivation and reinforce the desire to persist.

Another strategy is to keep the bigger picture in mind. Remembering why the habit was established in the first place and how it aligns with long-term goals can provide a powerful source of sustained motivation.

Case Studies of Individuals Who Successfully Maintained Their Good Habits Long-term

Learning from others who've successfully maintained good habits can be incredibly insightful. Consider the example of a professional athlete. They may have cultivated and maintained rigorous training and dietary habits over many years. One key to their success is consistency. They stick to their habits, even when it's challenging. They understand that progress isn't linear – there will be ups and downs, but the overall trajectory is what matters.

Another example could be a successful author who has maintained a habit of writing daily. They may not produce a masterpiece every day, but the consistent practice honed their skills and contributed to their long-term success. Their strategy often involves having a dedicated time and space for writing and making it a non-negotiable part of their day.

Both these examples highlight the importance of consistency, flexibility, and a clear connection between habits and long-term goals in maintaining good habits.

In conclusion, the long-term maintenance of good habits is a dynamic and ongoing process. It involves regular review and adjustment of habits, staying motivated, and learning from those who've successfully navigated this journey. With these strategies, anyone can not only establish but also maintain good habits over the long term.

Conclusion

The journey of breaking bad habits and forming good ones is a transformative process that can significantly impact your life. This guide has provided you with practical strategies, from setting SMART goals to maintaining consistency, overcoming challenges, and ensuring long-term maintenance of good habits. However, the real power of habit change lies not just in these strategies but in their application.

By now, you've understood that habits are more than just repetitive actions; they're the building blocks of your lifestyle. They influence your health, productivity, happiness, and overall well-being. Breaking detrimental habits and forming beneficial ones is an investment in yourself, a commitment to continual growth and improvement.

But remember, habit change isn't about perfection; it's about progress. It's about making small, consistent changes that add up over time. Don't be discouraged by setbacks or slow progress. Each step forward, no matter how small, is a victory.

Cultivating a growth mindset, staying motivated, and being flexible are key to this journey. Learning from the experiences of others who've successfully maintained their habits can also provide valuable insights and inspiration.

Now, it's your turn. You have the knowledge, the tools, and the strategies. All you need to do is take the first step. Start small, focus on one habit at a time, and be patient with yourself. The journey may be challenging, but it's also rewarding. And remember, you're not alone in this journey. There's a community of people out there, just like you, striving to better themselves through habit change.

So, start today. Begin your habit change journey. And as you progress, share your stories. Your successes, your challenges, your insights – they all matter. They can inspire others and provide valuable lessons. Plus, sharing your journey can also keep you accountable and motivated.

In the end, the journey of habit change is a personal one, but it's also a shared one. So, let's embark on this journey together, supporting and learning from each other along the way. After all, the journey towards becoming the best version of ourselves is the most rewarding journey we can undertake.

So, are you ready to start your habit change journey? Share your story, inspire others, and let's grow together.

FAQs

What is a habit?

A habit is a routine of behavior that is repeated regularly and tends to occur subconsciously. Habits can be either beneficial (like brushing your teeth every morning) or detrimental (like smoking).

How are habits formed?

Habits are formed through a process known as the habit loop, which consists of a cue, a routine, and a reward. The more this cycle is repeated, the more ingrained the habit becomes.

Why are habits important?

Habits are important because they shape our lives. Good habits can lead to success in various areas such as health, work, and relationships, while bad habits can hinder our progress and well-being.

Can habits be changed?

Yes, habits can be changed. While it requires effort and persistence, understanding the habit loop and consciously implementing changes can lead to the formation of new, healthier habits.

How long does it take to form a habit?

The duration required to establish a habit can differ significantly based on the individual, the behavior, and the situation. Typically, it ranges between 18 to 254 days to develop a consistent pattern of behavior.

What are some strategies for forming good habits?

Some strategies for forming good habits include setting clear and achievable goals, making the habit a daily one, starting with an easy habit, removing obstacles, and associating with people who have the habit you want to develop.

What's the role of willpower in habit formation?

Willpower plays a crucial role, especially in the initial stages of habit formation. However, once a habit becomes automatic, the reliance on willpower decreases. It's also important to note that willpower can be strengthened with regular practice.

Resources and Helpful Links

Parker-Pope, T. (2021, June 7). How to build healthy habits. *The New York Times.* https://www.nytimes.com/2020/02/18/well/mind/how-to-build-healthy-habits.html

Bad Habits: Definition, examples, and how to break them. (n.d.). The Berkeley Well-Being Institute. https://www.berkeleywellbeing.com/bad-habits.html

Manson, M. (2023, June 7). Creating Healthy Habits: A Practical guide. *Mark Manson.* https://markmanson.net/habits

Bhadraiah, P. (2023, May 11). *How to establish good and healthy habits and stick with them for the long term?* https://www.linkedin.com/pulse/how-establish-good-healthy-habits-stick-them-long-term-bhadraiah

PHPAdmin, B. (2020, August 25). *How to maintain health behaviours long term?* Practical Health Psychology. https://practicalhealthpsychology.com/2020/08/how-to-maintain-health-behaviours-long-term/

Cassandra. (2023, August 21). *The top 10 benefits of good habits.* Joyful Through It All. https://www.joyfulthroughitall.com/benefits-of-good-habits/

Herzliya Medical Center. (n.d.). *Bad habits and their impact on a human's health | Herzliya Medical Center | Treatment in Israel.* Herzliya Medical Center | Treatment in Israel.

https://hmcisrael.com/news/bad-habits-and-their-impact-on-a-humans-health/

Printed in Great Britain
by Amazon